The
SUPREME
WAY

The
SUPREME
WAY

Inner Teachings of the
Southern Mountain Tao

LOY CHING-YUEN

Translated with an introduction by
TREVOR CAROLAN and DU LIANG

NORTH ATLANTIC BOOKS

The Supreme Way

Published by
North Atlantic Books
P.O. Box 12327
Berkeley, CA 94712

Cover painting: *Cold Mountain*, 1993 by Arnold Shives
Cover and book design by Legacy Media, Inc.
Printed in the United States of America

The Supreme Way is sponsored by the Society for the Study of Native Arts and Sciences, a nonprofit educational corporation whose goals are to develop an educational and crosscultural perspective linking various scientific, social, and artistic fields; to nurture a holistic view of the arts, sciences, humanities, and healing; and to publish and distribute literature on the relationship of mind, body, and nature.

Library of Congress Cataloging-in-Publication Data
Loy, Ching-yuen, b. 1873.
　　　The supreme way : inner teachings of the Southern Mountain Tao /
translated by Trevor Carolyn and Du Liang.
　　　　　　　p. cm.
　　　Includes bibliographical references.
　　　ISBN 1-55643-239-9
　　　1. Tao.　2. Taoism.　3. Confucianism.　4. Buddhism—China.
I. Title.
B127.T3L69　1997
299'.514—dc21　　　　　　　　　96-39808
　　　　　　　　　　　　　　　　CIP

1 2 3 4 5 6 7 8 9 10 / 01 00 99 98 97

For the Venerable Ng Ching-Por, Sifu
in gratitude
And for his students Douglas Lau, Fred Young,
Jimmy & Jenny Chen and Alec & Soo-lan Ma
in the tradition

Contents

Translators' Introduction

Loy Ching-Yuen was born to a prosperous land-owning family in China's Hubei Province in 1873. He left home as a young man to study in seclusion with a Taoist master practicing a variety of traditional disciplines, including *Tai Chi Chuan, Chi Kung,* and naturopathic medicine.

We do not know at which mountain temple or with whom Master Loy studied, but the nature of his teachings handed down in *The Supreme Way* and *The Book of the Heart* fall within Taoism's *Yin* tradition. Loy's surviving students relate that he emphasized humility, self-study, self-discipline, and sitting meditation, the latter having a strong *Ch'an* (Zen) Buddhist orientation.

Loy Ching-Yuen returned to society at the request of his family, marrying and settling in the Shanghai area. In time, his skills as a healer and teacher were in considerable demand. An accomplished Taoist master noted for his cultivation of virtue "both within and without," Loy never established a formal center during his lengthy career. But he continued to enjoy a large following drawn from all spheres of society—unusual for the time as this cut through the rigid stratification of Chinese culture.

Generally consistent with teachings of the Ching Chung, "All Truth Dragon Gate" sect of Taoism which derives its lineage from Tang Dynasty master Lu Sun-Young, Master Loy's spiritual vision is also enriched in an exclusively Chinese fashion by both the

Buddha dharma and the basic tenets of Confucianism. Indeed, it can rightly be said that Loy Ching-Yuen's work embraces Buddhist, Taoist, and Confucian precepts without contradiction.

The Supreme Way is a manifestation of Loy Ching-Yuen's life-long dedication to the Taoist path, representing a further evolution of this modern master's determination to distill the teachings of China's great religions—Taoism, Confucianism, and Buddhism—into a spiritual vision transcending any single component. And there lies its appeal to significant numbers in the West, for although an ever increasing audience is attracted to the perennial wisdom of the East, many people encounter difficulty in embracing the highly idiosyncratic practices associated with traditional Asian religions.

The following pages are a record of Master Loy's lectures, compiled at Chongqing in 1948 during the chaotic Chinese civil war by his disciple Hanxu. In a brief preface to the original Chinese edition, Hanxu remarks as dramatically as any lover of fiction might wish:

> *I had lived in this mortal world more than*
> *thirty years and was afflicted with hopes and*
> *desires from which I could not release myself.*
> *My energies and intelligence were decaying.*
> *One day I woke suddenly and felt a fear so*
> *strong that I became determined to abandon*
> *the things which consumed my body and heart,*
> *and to look for the meaning of life and the*
> *great Tao.*

He goes on to relate that after unsuccessfully dogging the Master's footsteps for two years, first in Shanghai, then in Chongqing, Loy Ching-Yuen finally accepted him as a student conditional upon Hanxu's compilation of a record of Master Loy's teachings for the benefit of other students. *The Supreme Way* is that book.

Customarily, Taoist teaching is transmitted orally in the manner of Asia's timeless student/master tradition. But for any number of reasons—perhaps the cataclysmic civil war then raging throughout China was a major consideration—Loy Ching-Yuen chose to leave written word of his Taoist lore, knowledge, and practice. And it is considerable. Those familiar with his *Book of the Heart** know of his depth and acuity of vision. *The Supreme Way* offers us a further, more expansive glimpse into the profound mystery of Tao/Buddha mind, also providing a useful historical context in which to place its discussion of China's three great spiritual traditions. This context is important, for Master Loy's intent from the outset of the book is to present us with the development of Taoism's innermost teachings.

One point should be clear. The Taoism discussed here is not that of popular imagination. There are no magical elixirs here, no alchemy, tantrism or other mantic arts. Such pursuits came into vogue long after the flowering of true Taoism, and at best they represent a particularly degenerate form of Taoist practice. Rather, what is recognized here is the spiritual principle outlined by Lao-tzu in his Book of Morals, the *Tao Te Ching*—"that which existed before heaven and earth; that dominates all things, and that does not decline with the seasons." It is the ineffable, of course, that which Lao-tzu himself proclaimed cannot be named. Yet, as other sages have allowed—Shakyamuni and Confucius among them—it is useful to have the appropriate words to hand when educating others in the correct paths by which the suffering and ignorance of this world may be overcome.

∞

The Supreme Way of the book's title refers to the *Tao*, or the Way of Heaven that existed before Lao-tzu, *before* all memorable sages. We may know it as the perfection of the wisdom to which China's three great religions aspired, each in its own fashion—a wisdom attainable only be overcoming the limitations of any single exclusive

*Trans. by T. Carolan & B. Chen; Shambhala, 1990.

vision—or we may know it as "the Tao which cannot be named," that transcends the wisdom of any one spiritual path. But whatever our interpretation, at bottom the Supreme Way is none other than the profound mystery of unvarnished, unblemished Buddha/Taomind.

∞

In addition to his own Taoist training, Loy Ching-Yuen's long period of study gave him a profound understanding of both Buddhism and Confucianism. Recognizing the spiritual calamity of the age about him, Loy sought an efficient means by which the mysteries of self-realization could be explained in simple terms. By delineating a path embracing the larger truths of Confucianism, Buddhism, and Taoism, he presents us with insights drawn from a deep understanding of self-nature, and a book bearing witness to a lineage of great teachers and great wisdom books.

The Supreme Way is clear and consistent in its manifestation of how China's three great religious traditions have co-existed for the better part of two thousand years, and how each has brought its own gift of knowledge to our understanding of the human condition. Its presentation of the process of higher Taoist meditation practice is occasionally quite breath-taking. Its explanations of Buddhism's central concept of compassion and of Confucianism's core idea of humanism are concretely delineated. Indeed, as chapters progress, Master Loy's interfused ideas and practices from the three great teachings remind one of the veracity of the great Buddhist text the *Avatamsaka*, or Flower Adornment Sutra. In its luminous image of Indra's all-encompassing world net of mirrors, each reflects back upon the other in a central phrasing of all creation's interbeing and interpenetration.

That is the Supreme Way: the central Taoist/Buddhist image of unity, of Oneness, which realized brings us back to wholeness with creation. Yet as Master Loy informs, while we achieve this return to wholeness through practice, there is no set practice. Self-realization turns out to be, as Lao-tzu first informs, no special thing: Practice—be it *zazen* sitting meditation, physical training, or gardening has as its ultimate end, simply Ordinary Mind. The challenge of remaining mindful in all our undertakings rests on attunement, tolerance, and perseverance.

The Supreme Way offers substantial, meaningful insight into China's three great spiritual traditions. It is a little masterpiece in many ways, with much to discover among its pages for which we may be deeply grateful.

Concerning the text, Pinyin (romanized Mandarin Chinese) equivalents have been used for all proper names, other than those for which traditional Wade-Giles usage is now convention (Lao-tzu, Chuang-tzu, Confucius, Shakyamuni, etc.). Footnotes have been added where they may be of help in clarifying historical or personal information. The italicized verse fragments that conclude each chapter are intended to be chanted.

"Confucianism" as it is employed throughout refers to a body of theory that evolved over many hundreds of years, not simply to the widely known works of Confucius himself. "Buddhism" refers in the main to Chinese Buddhism, although readers will note further discussion of this subject in Chapter Three.

The following translation is collaborative and loyal in spirit, if not always in precise linguistic nature, to the original. Frederick Young offered invaluable insight and corrections throughout for which we are especially grateful. To our wives Kwangshik and Wun Pin; to our children; and to all those who contributed in a dozen different ways,

Nine Bows.

Trevor Carolan & Du Liang
Deep Cove, British Columbia

Preface to the Original Chinese Edition

As Lao-tzu says, "Tao can be explained, but not with ordinary words." Hence, *the Way* that can be explained is necessarily different from that which cannot. If we think of Tao in terms of everyday experience, however, and of the knowledge that comes to us through the observation of a meditative practice, then the Way begins to take form.

Between heaven and humanity, between the internal and external worlds of imagination and reality, exists a world of dualities: objective and subjective, the obvious and the ambiguous, prosperity and decay. Here, the phenomena of cause and effect are manifest.

Tao—the Way—is unblemished, empty, and boundless. All things begin and end with its Unity. Confucians have long conceived of this Unity throughout their philosophy. Likewise, Buddhists conclude that all worldly manifestations are fundamentally One; and for their part, Taoists hold resolutely to the concept of Oneness. Unity is the key to the ten thousand things.

Master Loy's *Book of the Supreme Way* defers to numerous teachings in its search for answers into the nature of the world. Forged from the teachings of China's three great religious paths in a way neither flowery nor colorful, this book's assertions are profound. For indeed, it is a private treasure and those who read this book will not waste time in their search for the true path.

Master Loy was born in Zhongzhou, where there is rich soil and abundant water. His beliefs are of Taoism's Southern Mountain tradition, and their goal is to lead us to the Virtuous Realm. As humanity follows the way of earth, and earth the way of heaven, so heaven follows the Supreme Way, and the Way follows what is natural. It is known that they have their reasons. So we must ask, who could write such a book but a wise and moral person?

The Disciples
Hanxu, Chao Yu-Xiu,
Yang Yongkang, Yinfang

Mid-Spring, 1953
Wuhua Mountain, China

The
SUPREME
WAY

CHAPTER ONE

"Three-in-One": The Roots and Nature of China's Three Great Spiritual Traditions

Since the earliest times, before creation, a great *Tao*—a Way, or Source—has existed that harmonizes the balance of *Yin* and Yang, and which cultivates all things under heaven.

In the beginning there were no religions. Then, as humanity increased in size, competitive and harsh behaviors emerged. The Sages were obliged to conceive ways by which social harmony could be maintained and abuses prevented. Various faiths established themselves in response to the different needs of race, custom, language, and territory. In China three great doctrines arose, instructing their followers in how to better the world after the examples of Lao-tzu, Confucius, and the Buddha Shakyamuni.

As these teachers passed from the world, their disciples recorded the teachings and doctrines left them by the Masters, often adding further learned commentaries to them. In this way the original teachings were preserved and transmitted from generation to generation. In time, however, the language used in explaining the original doctrines became more and more complicated, and commentaries on the great teachings grew beyond number.

As communication and trade evolved, Buddhism from India mingled with both the Confucianism and Taoism of China. In some respects, China's original paths had already exerted influence upon each other; but in spite of these developments, many believers held unyieldingly to the principles of their original faiths, and points of divergence appeared among the three religions. In time, these arguments grew in severity and sectarian biases flourished, though this was never intended by the great Teachers themselves.

Time passes. In our present age we have grown conscious of the error of denying one another's teachings. The task of reconciliation, of concord, is paramount. This realization of the importance of learning from one another, and of the impossibility of enlightening all humanity through any one spiritual vision alone, also enables us to embrace common bonds in our efforts to achieve cooperative goals.

Originally, human communication was poor: people had only limited knowledge. Life was leaner, more economical, less complex. Men and women worked for their food and clothing only, surviving without high material expectation or desire. The world was calmer. People had not yet begun to torment each other with sophisticated ideas. In some ways it was an idyllic age.

As society developed from tribal and clan structures to that of the state, stratification appeared among peoples. Struggles among individuals and classes evolved within the state, and among competing cities and nations from without. The means of war and conflict were refined—first through intelligence and cunning, then through weaponry and language. The more human society progressed, it seemed, the more suffering increased.

∞

As the sages teach, the great Tao and the universe appeared together, regulating all things. Followed wisely by society, the Way offers guidance in accordance with the demands of particular circumstances and needs. It is of aid in the ajudication of justice, fairness, equality, and compassion. Buddhism, Taoism, and Confucianism share a common source in this original path of truth, so it may reward us to consider the development of their various individual principles and applications.

Among followers of Confucius, the principles of Humanism and Loyalty serve as guiding ideals. Buddhists find similar inspiration in their belief in Compassion and Taking Refuge. Taoists, for their part, revere the elemental mystery and ambiguity of Nature.

Customarily, Confucianism's chief ideals of loyalty and humanism are amplified through its cardinal expressions of filial piety and self-purification. Similarly, the Buddhist roots of compassion and mercy are also tempered by the "four forms and four manifestations,"* whereas Taoism complements its faith in primal mystery with belief in *Wu-wei*—the appropriate utility of nonresistance. Formally, while each faith has its own expression, sense of purpose, and individual characteristics, on examination they each share certain fundamentally related spiritual principles.

We must not forget that Confucian tenets emphasize the expression of "good-heartedness," of goodwill toward the world, and that this suggests men and women are to be treated equally, without favor. In this it does not differ radically from the Buddhist principle of compassion for all living things, or from Taoism's advocacy of temperance in all worldly affairs. Moreover, if as the Sages tell us, material objects that can be made by human hands are believed ultimately not to exist as independent phenomena—if the things we strive for cannot ultimately be possessed—then we must inquire into the purpose or utility of exclusivity, competitiveness, or divisiveness among followers of differing faiths.

The true purpose of religion is to teach us how to serve and better the world. Confucius pointedly instructs that only through humanism and loyalty to ideals and ethics can we become virtuous. Buddhists know this well, treating others compassionately, for they understand that as mortals we are all vulnerable to temptation. Taoists too, in their devotion to the mystery of the Middle Way,

---

* The "four forms" denote Divergence, Synthesis, Compliance, and Non-Compliance. The "four manifestations" are Unborn (Pre-conscious, or "No") Mind, Motivation, Obduracy, and Egoism.

believe we must detach ourselves from extremes of passionate nature, good or ill.

A spiritual path of life, whatever its philosophical origin, offers us the real possibility of embracing higher realms of self-awareness. We should be mindful, therefore, of attunement to our place within nature. Let us remember that the Celestial Realm of Heaven is not reserved simply for a chosen few; it is available to us all equally.

Accordingly, we must be attentive in the correction of our individual faults and be mindful of our responsibilities to the world and to others. Is this not enlightenment of a kind?

> *The Sages teach a way of attainment.*
> *Though their paths may vary,*
> *The one source remains the same.*
> *Imbued with their knowledge and wisdom,*
> *We may achieve our goal of the Virtuous*
> *Realm.*

CHAPTER TWO

The Way of Tao

Taoism is unique in that a lengthy vacuum exists in history between the time of Lao-tzu's writing his *Tao Te Ching* and its growth as a popular religious path—as if, one might say, a mighty dragon's head had existed without a tail for many generations. While other renowned masters such as Chuang-tzu (Zhuangzi) and Lieh-tzu inherited and further developed the richness of Lao-tzu's guiding thought through parable and commentary in the master's own profound tradition, it was not until the scholarly gathering of the *Huainanzi* following the Han Dynasty that a systematized method of Taoist ritual and practice was initiated. Only with this creation of a formal doctrine did Taoism begin its steady growth.

Large numbers of books came to address the Tao as a subject, although of the thousands that have been written, none betters the *Tao Te Ching*. Tragically, Lao-tzu passed away without the opportunity of personally teaching a group of followers, yet students of Taoism have learned from his written word through countless generations, and his greatness remains undiminished.

Of the many misperceptions the world has had of Taoism, the most prominent concerns its methods of transmission from teacher to student. Taoism has customarily been taught in relative secrecy at calm, remote locations. It relies on oral transmission from

---

* The Huainanzi (Huai-nan tzu): a scholarly gathering of commentaries from the reign of Liu An, King of Huai-nan, (approx. 125 B.C.).

teacher to student, emphasizing firstly the purification of one's environment, and secondly, detachment from the outside world.

Since Taoism does not profess itself publically, its essentials may seem hard to grasp; it is perennially accused of being reluctant to disclose its knowledge, but this is not necessarily so. We must remember that Lao-tzu's original teaching is concerned not with the individual but with the ineffable—"that which cannot be known."

When Chuang-tzu and Lieh-tzu wrote, they were influenced largely by Lao-tzu's impersonal vision. Following the Han and Jin Dynasties, however, Taoist commentaries began propagating a formal doctrine. Later, during Taoism's fertile Tang and Five Kingdoms Dynasty period, many great teachers arose, leaving behind a legacy of knowledge and historical lore.

Many of these teachers lived secluded in the mountains away from the outer, material world, and anecdotes concerning their lives grew and flourished with time. These were sages who contemplated Tao's inner mysteries for years, who were selective in their choice of students, and who chose only those students whom they knew to be of sufficient patience and virtue. These students were guided by their masters to the higher gates of Taoism, and in time they themselves taught others. Taoist influence increased naturally in this way until it became an independent school.

By the early Sung Dynasty, Taoist temples could be found all over China, and through newfound imperial support, Taoism temporarily eclipsed the dominant position of Buddhism. While it enjoyed its greatest popularity during this period, Taoism also fell prey to institutional excesses, for as larger numbers came to embrace its teachings and live in its temples, bureaucratic practices grew. Students taught by masters whose own practice had grown corrupt gradually fell prey to the attractions of superstition and the mystical arts, and to using them as a means of exalting their position. Such occurrences were not uncommon among various Buddhist communities either, although such behavior was a shameful betrayal of the founding teachings of both Shakyamuni and Lao-tzu.

During the Sung period, Taoism divided into what were known as the Temple and Mountain schools, with the former noted for its community institutions and rituals. The latter proved attractive principally to independent scholars who had wearied of Taoism's growing formalism.

Living in remote fastnesses, followers of the Mountain School withdrew from the outer world. Distaining wealth and reputation, they were devoted to ardent spiritual practice, some in solitude, others among like-minded companions, for it became customary in the Mountain tradition that with the attainment of high skill in one's path of practice, one then re-embraced the external world through the acceptance of disciples.

Temple doctrine meanwhile emphasized forms of aesthetic expression such as the writing of textual commentaries, establishment of monastic rules, study of the celestial arts, and the casting of oracles. While these pursuits have merit, they were nevertheless considered "empty forms" by those of the Mountain School who chose to spend their days observing the natural world and striving to similarly attune their own self-nature. The Mountain School represented a profoundly spiritual practice, and we may attribute the longevity of Taoism's vision to the work of its adherents.

Differences of practice also existed within the Mountain School—differences in skill, forms, and understanding. Taoists lived in different environments and lived separate experiences, which naturally influenced the wisdom of their respective paths.

The most serious point of dissension arose between the Northern and Southern branches of the Mountain School. The Northern branch viewed nature-wisdom as the starting point of practice. Taking calmness and emptiness as their guiding principles, they believed that the cultivation of quietude was the appropriate method of knowing the fullness of Tao. Northerners accepted that the contemplative observance of nature-wisdom was life's optimum foundation.

Conversely, the Southern branch viewed life itself as the starting point. Its practitioners emphasized the training of a healthy physical body through the practice of various dynamic exercises. With the body—the foundation of life—correctly strengthened, they believed it possible to fully cultivate one's inner nature through the cultivation of wisdom and compassion.

Initially, the two branches shared similar perspectives; their only difference lay in the expression of practice. But as time passed, they grew incompatible.

In reality, there is no difference between the two. In order to truly master the great Way, followers of the Northern branch—the school of nature-wisdom—must naturally strengthen their bodies. And for Taoists of the Southern branch to truly refine and purify their bodies, they must similarly attune to the wisdom of nature to reach the same sublime state of emptiness desired by their Northern cousins. The problem here is not one of doctrine but of incomplete practice. Lineage, school, or sect aside, it is our physical and intellectual beings which we must harmonize. Followers of Northern branch Mountain Tao must take care that their love of nature observance is not cultivated merely intellectually to the detriment of their physical condition, while those of the Southern branch must be mindful that their intense training of the physical body is not cultivated at the expense of human compassion or kindliness in daily life.

The true Way has but one path and there should be no superficial differences between schools. We should take advantage of being attentive to all schools of thought and to all approaches. Lao-tzu himself, it seems, predicted that his followers would separate into different camps, and for this reason he gave us the unsurpassable principle of "Holding to the One."*

The true path encourages us to follow the Way of Heaven, and its highest expression—the Supreme Way—is in the understanding of pre-reflective, unborn consciousness. Following the will of heaven, we must be purposeful in holding to the unity of this great Oneness and Emptiness.

This perfection of "the uncarved block" or "the unshaped, unformed, unborn" is specifically emphasized here because it is the key to all Taoist doctrine. If we can empty our heart and meditate mindfully upon this we will have achieved a great deal.

> *Though different, the Northern and*
> *Southern branches are ultimately One.*
> *Within them lie the keys to the gate,*
> *to the unbound, unborn state.*
> *Let this be known.*

* This principle is discussed comprehensively in Chapter Six.

CHAPTER THREE

Concerning the Buddha Dharma

Buddhism first appeared in China during the Eastern Jin Dynasty
(A.D. 317–419) when monks arrived from India carrying sacred texts
of the Buddha dharma. Eventually, these texts were translated into
Chinese. Among early translators, the labors of Kumolosi of the
Yaogin era (A.D. 384–417) and Xuan Zhuang of the Tang Dynasty
(A.D. 670–905) are seminal.

Translations of Buddhist scriptures spread steadily throughout
China. Consequently, the body and richness of the Buddha's teachings became more widely available. Temples were built throughout
the country, and interest in the monkhood flourished. This flowering was actively encouraged by emperors and court officials to the
extent that gradually Buddhism began to dominate China's intellectual climate.

The arrival of Buddhism satisfied an urgent demand of the times.
Critical social ideas are always based on a historical synergy, and cri-
sis situations influence the acceptance of any new knowledge.
Following the Three Kingdoms period (A.D. 220–280) people suf-
fered from a spiritual malaise: old ideas, it seemed, were incapable
of eliminating injustice or regulating a rampant desire for material
prosperity. Guidance and redemption were needed among the people. On its arrival, the Buddha dharma was welcomed; easily
embraced, its growth among the Chinese was as effortless and nat-

ural as the echo of a mountain valley. During this time, Confucianism was in serious decline.

Internal warfare was rampant; Taoism had yet to thrive; people lived in an abyss of misery. Buddhism won people's hearts with its profound wisdom and doctrine of mercy and compassion.

Buddhism was easily and popularly embraced by the people because it accepts all seekers regardless of status or background. Unlike other faiths, Buddhism focuses sharply upon present life— *here and now*—and its broad vision embraces everything within the cosmos, including the realms of plant and animal life.

Buddhist doctrine is sufficiently rich that it cannot be easily summarized. While we are only discussing the Buddha dharma's general principles and applications here, we should note, however, its emphasis on detachment from the illusions of the external world, and its instruction to forego lust and extremes of desire in adhering to the Buddha's Eightfold Path.

Buddhist scriptures were originally written in Sanskrit and Pali, and their Chinese translations were usually crafted into classical Chinese. Ordinary monks could seldom completely understand this script, however, and even solitary mystics skilled in the classics likely experienced difficulty in understanding the sacred texts. Nor were Buddhist scriptures as widely available as their Confucian counterparts, and given this situation it is understandable that Buddhist masters were obliged to instruct and practice their rites as best as they were able wherever and whenever opportunity allowed. Inevitably, different teachers employed different approaches, and their explanations naturally generated different degrees of understanding among Buddhist students. The result was that some schools and traditions remained simple while others grew deep; some survived, others withered and failed.

Although Buddhism's various schools continue to hold to their own doctrines and practices, they exist together agreeably, unlike many schools of Confucianism. Among Chinese Buddhists,

Ch'anzong (*Ch'an*, or Zen) and *Jintuzong* are most widespread. Most monks devote themselves to *Ch'anzong*; solitary hermits generally to *Jintuzong*. There is also a lesser-known school, *Shizong*, which tends to focus only on doctrine, less on practice. And recently *Mizong* (Vajrayana), brought to China by Tibetans, has grown in popularity. Emphasizing liturgy, sutra-chanting, and the mantic arts, its complex doctrines are steeped in mystery.

Originally, Buddhism and Taoism were regarded as being without major contradiction, and Taoist and Buddhist temples existed together throughout China. Happily, since followers of each faith were not obliged to attack or persecute each other, both Buddhism and Taoism found their own constituency and in this way they thrived.

We must note as well that both Buddhism and Taoism embrace compassion and equality as guiding principles, and that both employ the image of emptiness as a unifying central concept. Like Buddhists, who strive to become Buddhas, so Taoists in similar fashion strive to become Celestial.

Indeed, Buddhism shares many deep similarities with Taoism. The sitting meditation of *Ch'anzong*, and *Mizong's* practice of energy transmission are similar to the sitting practice and heart-training methods of the Mountain School's Northern branch of Taoism. And while Buddhism and Taoism may pursue somewhat different ends, each shares as a beginning place the essential idea that worldly distraction must be overcome in order to transcend the negative aspects of human existence.

Buddhists, however, treasure the soul while looking down on the body; Taoists believe we must cultivate Tao-nature through the body until our soul detaches from it naturally. And while Buddhists strive to discard the false self of the body and attach importance only to the eternal soul, Taoists consider soul and body as one—each element of this duality being equally capable of transcendence.

Both Buddhism and Taoism enlighten us with the profound teaching of detachment and emptiness—*Shunyata*. We must only be willing to embark upon the merciful vessel and take refuge. Humanity is fortunate the doors to these two great paths are open to all.

> *The Buddha way is endless:*
> *No Self, no Other.*
> *At last, we find ourselves in the Western*
> *Paradise.*
> *Samsara is essential in the Karma of our*
> *three lives.*
> *This present life is but ambiguity:*
> *The way of Nature guides us through.*

---

* Previous, present, and future lives

CHAPTER FOUR

"The Great Harmony of Confucius"

Confucianism is China's oldest ordered system of human structural relationships. Historically, as Chinese society evolved, its cultural expression could be fully observed and documented. Observations of this nature were first recorded by King Chou,* and his knowledge of history, ritual, science, politics, and the arts served as the original source material of Master Kung's (Confucius') own philosophical inquiries.

King Chou's early observations are elaborated upon constantly throughout Confucius' celebrated works. Indeed, Master Kung's lifelong search for the human individual's appropriate place and responsibility within society relies upon the examples set by "ancients" such as King Chou. Confucianism itself, though, is not confined exclusively to the thoughts of Master Kung or his teachers. Its formal content also includes the deliberations of other scholars such as Mencius (Menzi) and Xunzi (Hsun Tzu), who contributed significantly to the ethical and moral canons of Confucianism.

Confucius was a product of the warring, feudal times which gave him inspiration, and his founding principles are the maintenance of social order and stability. Originally conceived as a system of individual guidance founded on the rectification and purification of

---

* Founder of the Chou Dynasty (1122–255 B.C.). Confucius began his scholarly career as a clerk in the memorial temple of the Duke of Chou, a descendent of the founding King.

one's inner heart, Confucianism's focus of attention upon the balance of inner and external harmony expands to encompass one's primary personal relationships within family, state, and the cosmos. Confucianism's finely wrought vision offers a precise, idealized framework for living, and its influence has been monumental.

The formal content of Confucianism is comprised of four elements: its fundamental principles of order and virtue; the internalization and the externalization of these principles; and the specific applications of the principles.

Internalization is the study and acceptance of things as *they are*. This condition of acceptance obliges deep honesty as to one's personal intentions, for it is worldly intentions and motivations that most affect the purity of our heart, our inner self. It is believed that from this beginning place of acceptance we may proceed with the rectification of our personal and family life.

Externalization implies the establishing of greater degrees of harmony within our closest family relationships. By projecting or externalizing our own inner harmony outwardly to others, we gradually bring to a correct state of order various other worldly and spiritual relationships—those involving state and the cosmos—"after the example of the ancients."

Confucianism is guided by the principles of Humanism and Virtue (Loyalty), and their application is best witnessed within the various hierarchical expressions of familial piety. It is these essential expressions of faithfulness, loyalty, and tolerance within the family structure that are subsequently extended into the state's political and social hierarchies.

Confucianism's traditionally strong emphasis on education derives from its concern in particular with relationships within the social hierarchy. The education of the less privileged in knowledge of religious and communal rituals, ethics, and the arts is believed to be an essential element of successful social organization. Ideally, Confucianism should be flexible in its outlook, recognizing that methods of instruction must change in accordance with the times, locality, and governing political circumstance.

Confucian theories were specifically founded on the ideal of developing both a more enlightened human being and a better human society. Confucius himself believed that lasting peace can only be achieved by societies founded on moral, humanistic foundations. But while acknowledging that differences exist within humanity—between educated and ignorant, noble and poor, virtuous and corrupt—Confucianism in practice has regrettably not been successful in detaching itself from the inequities of social hierarchies, and its main ideas have been closely associated with those of the governors—to the neglect of larger elements of society. Confucian theory does, however, criticize unjust behavior and harsh politics, and it takes pains not to dismiss the less privileged. In particular, it delineates the six *Fu*, three *Shi*, and four *Wei*,* to encourage correct behavior.

Confucianism expresses a further great ideal which it seeks to effect within human society through the mindful application of its principles. In form, this idea may be compared with democracy, considered a treasure of the West, although aesthetically it is closer to Lao-tzu's concept of "profound morality," or Mencius' idea of "universal goodwill." Accepting that class differences do exist, Confucianism regards every laborer as a useful contributor to society. No occupation is regarded as being without merit. Confucius was devoted to the common good, and this belief in the importance of human dignity represents a very significant component of Confucianism.

A primary emphasis is also placed by Confucian followers on inner calmness, and the fundamental gesture in attaining this state

---

* The six Fu were ancient China's principal departments of government; the three Shi are terms expressing correct morality, emphasis on practical results, and goodwill toward others. The four *Wei* are terms depicting manners and customs, human ties, sense of honor, and sense of shame.

of harmony is the purification of our heart and the practice of mind-fulness. As Zhu Xi observes in the *Da Xue*,* as seekers we invari-ably experience difficulty in finding the beginning place of our spiritual journey. Indeed, he relates that it is easier to detect false or discouraging signs along the way. But entry and progress to high-er realms compel us to follow an initiatory path: self-realization can-not be accomplished otherwise. Zhu Xi's teaching affirms that we must each discover our own entranceway by devoting ourselves attentively to a way of practice, thereby discovering the nature and limits of the correct path, imbuing it with an abiding love for others.

Self-realization in the Confucian sense remains an intensely per-sonal engagement—something invariably misunderstood by those unfamiliar with its doctrines. The sages have always taught that the only means to true self-realization is through detachment from external bonds, and this has long been a singular element of Confucian principle.

Other aspects of Confucian philosophy also address the nature of human existence. Gao Zi** addressed this matter, and it has been studied repeatedly by Confucian scholars throughout the ages, although it is likely to continue perplexing "pure" scholars. Nature and Tao are also discussed in Zhu Xi's *Da Xue*, and Mencius address-es the matter, though not at length. It is noteworthy that during the enlightened, materialistic Sung era that Confucians conceived of life and nature as one, much as in Buddhism, but an original Confucian understanding is now regrettably vague.

A question lingers: What of those uninterested in or immune to spiritual rectification? Does Confucianism offer a solution? To this end, the legalist Xunzi created the School of Laws *(Fa)*, advocating the use of regulatory law as a means of problem-solving. Yet not even perfect laws can cover every human eventuality; people grow

* The Da Xue, written by the neo-Confucian Zhu Xi of the Sung Dynasty (A.D. 960–1278), explicates various aspects of Confucian theory.

** The Confucian philosopher Gao Zi revised certain aspects of Confucian knowl-edge, but he is incompletely recorded in historical records.

more clever, they may cheat, find loopholes, destroy and abuse both the law and society. Confucius taught that it was only when "good men lost the power to influence society that laws would be needed at all." Saints are few in number; virtue is not normally found in abundance; the world is composed of the commonplace after all, hence Confucianism has always emphasized the thorough grounding of both the individual and society in a sound, moral education.

The Confucian path seeks a harmonious world;
Its followers pursue tranquility and purification.
To bring the world to order,
the key is action.
Mindful of the great mystery of Tao,
Our practice must accord with nature.

CHAPTER FIVE

Essentials of Mindful Practice

Buddhists, Confucians, and Taoists alike favor quiet, individual meditation as an essential means of practice. Successful meditation begins with three basic conditions: belief, perseverance, and willpower. Only through mastering each step can we experience the deeper richness of meditation's form and content.

Progress in mastering belief, perseverance, and willpower is like climbing rugged mountain peaks: courage is needed to reach the highest heights. Like an oarsman boating through white-water, our practice must be attentive, without hesitation; otherwise we may sink through carelessness.

∞

Meditation consists of both internal and external practice. Internal practice in particular is the very foundation of Taoism, for it purifies our inner nature, tempering the will and detaching our emotions from the material world. It must be attentively focused, without carnal, worldly, or malicious thought.

External meditative practice must also be mindfully observed, for it consists of service to others in alleviating suffering in the world. Practically, this extends to offering help to those with disabilities, to the oppressed and hopeless, to those suffering from disease. Such work may be undertaken, either directly or indirectly, through personal labor or philanthropic work.

External practice reinforces internal meditation, shaping "Taoist Mind" and increasing our effectiveness in the world. Equally important as our inner practice, it cannot be separated from it, and this should not be forgotten. The principle of caring for others is evoked by conscience and the demands of humanity, for when the righteous sense need among the people they must seek to satisfy it.

Helping others, we should not then regard ourselves as having done anything special. It is better to forget such sentiment by not allowing it into our heart, where it may complicate our thoughts. The thirst for recognition is incompatible with Tao.

⚬

Internal meditative practice has two components: the passive and the active forms, each of which should be properly mastered. These forms are like *yin* and *yang;* the former being passive, the latter active. Such dualities must co-exist harmoniously since everything under heaven flows from them. Within our bodies *yin* and *yang* must also complement each other so that our energy and circulation are fully maximized, balanced, and in continuous harmony. Masters of the healing arts know this to be true, hence it must not be forgotten.

Practice of both active and passive forms of meditation should be regularized in order to achieve the optimum benefit of such exercise. Passive (or sitting) meditation should be followed by dynamic exercise such as *Tai Chi* or *Chi Kung,* then by further sitting meditation. Our personal energy is certain to be increased through this method; however, there is one operative condition. Whether active or passive, meditation must be practiced fully and naturally. For instance, during sitting meditation we do not simply sit; we focus mindfully on precisely what it is we are engaged in. And in active meditation such as physical training, we must avoid being perfunctory about our movements: we must learn to move our inner energy. Our attention must not be distracted; action should be fluid, detached from thought.

Active and passive meditation are in fact one and the same. Each subsumes the other; dynamic meditation incorporates the passive and vice versa.

Passive meditation is often misunderstood. Here we must center our *chi*, or energy, allowing it to circulate naturally throughout the body via the bloodstream and vital meridians without obstruction. This phenomenon is experienced only after long, diligent practice.

Successful sitting meditation relies upon three essentials. First, we must dismiss any external thoughts or desires from our mind: our inner space must be as unblemished as crystal. Second, we must concentrate upon our inner self, ensuring we remain still and empty. Third, we must block any external or internal distractions as they arise in the mind to avoid disruption of our inner quietude. These three steps are a trinity and cannot be separated. If followed correctly and regularly they afford heart and mind deep and abiding pleasure.

⸎

Dynamic meditation also relies upon three essentials, each of which must be developed and mastered over time. The first two are external—the movement of head, neck, and upper body, and the motion of limbs and torso. The third stage relies upon internal training, in developing the circulation of our *chi* and blood. Proper coordination of these three essentials is critical and should not be approached haphazardly. Skill should be attained in the first and second stages before attempting mastery of the third. This is the unifying means by which we store *chi* in our bones, nourish the skin with healthy blood, and decrease calcification of the major joints. It is one of the dynamic path's more profound mysteries, and within it lies the secret to relaxation of our complete physical being.

It must be noted that one aspect of meditation practice is unconditional: be it dynamic, passive, internal, or external, fully realized meditation is dependent on the discarding of any desire for material gain. Wherever we are, we must see the place we practice as the Mountain, for although we are not obliged to pursue a life of monastic

solitude, we must discard our passions at the entranceway to our place of meditation. The Supreme Way is the path of detachment.

Self-illumination during meditation remains a profoundly mysterious experience, an unseen phenomenon not easily understood by those without some experience of the meditative process themselves. Nevertheless, traces of the immanence, the godliness of the still moment experienced during successful meditation are readily observable in the natural world by anyone caring to see.

The path of meditative practice familiarizes us with primordial consciousness. We learn in time that Tao, the unborn state, is the Way; that Tao-mind, like Buddha-mind, is the recognition of there being no "otherness;" only our own complete absorption within the Great Wheel, within its manifold, ceaselessly changing nature.

The Way is endless
Yet mindful practice brings calm and order.
With perseverance and determination
Our belief is firm.
Internal, external, the dynamic, and passive,
The path is harmonious,
Detaching Self mindfully
from the world.

CHAPTER SIX

Embracing Oneness

Unbound, unborn nature—the uncorrupted mystery of the uncarved block—has been discussed earlier, but to avoid confusion on this point it is useful for us to have a beginning place of reference. We may consider the great Tao as having two essential components: Truth and Primal Unity.

The embracing of Truth—the truth of *What Is*—is the critical means by which self-realization is achieved. Embracing truth, we link heaven and heart, for truth is the Ultimate: the Great Wisdom. All incontestable and constant faces of nature, all existent things, all visible and immortal purposes are embodied within it. Truth is the measure of human action: its manifestations are universal and limitless.

Adherence steadfastly to the Truth is a necessary condition for entrance to the realm of the immortals—a profundity which can neither be understood nor researched half-heartedly. The Truth is something we realize through sincerity, and through continuous, faithful practice. It is never far from hand, and its mystery is a matter of attuning ourselves to greater awareness of our place in the world.

Truth can also be expressed in terms of Energy—the primal energy of heaven which cultivates all things. Embracing the Supreme Way, we may utilize its power within our lives against negative forces, yet energy is an ambiguous phenomenon; without perceivable form it is generated within the body through mastery of various forms of practice or training which lead ultimately to the discovery of Self, and to the greater powers that exist beyond.

Truth can also be understood through Emptiness, a treasured word in both Taoism and Buddhism. All things of this world are rooted in Emptiness and subsumed by it. We need not fear this: we need not regard the idea with suspicion, for emptiness is something experienced gently and willingly in meditation. Buddhism and Taoism encourage this as a means of stilling the mind and overcoming human anxiety. By cultivating emptiness inwardly, meditation practice and similar training methods develop us to higher levels where mind detaches from self and ego in embracing the great Void itself.

Truth is also known through *Spirit*. Whatever their nature, all things endowed with wisdom have spirit. This element should be nurtured within both mind and body over longer and longer periods of time, an action which serves to purify our body and the universe as well, keeping them sacred.

Although truth may be understood through the expressions of energy, emptiness, and spirit, it must be conceived of as a distinct reality if we are to realize its power. Knowledge of the oneness of truth's component parts ensures us entrance to the gates of Tao.

∞

Lao-tzu spoke of Oneness many times, for example, in "engaging the spirit with Oneness," or "to obtain Oneness, become one with All," and again, "the sage holds to the One." What he refers to, of course, are ways of practice. His purpose in such references and parables is to guide us in the linking up of heaven and heart. Lao-tzu knew clearly that both beginning and end are One, and that all things—the ten thousand dharmas, as the Buddhists relate—evolve from the One same source. *Yin* and *yang* the four seasons, the eight primary symbols of the *I Ching*—all are based on the primal unity of Oneness.

Now it does not matter to which religion we adhere: in every case we must follow the principle of holding to the One. Confucianism, Taoism, and Buddhism all meld easily with the doctrine of Oneness; nothing of substance can be mastered without the discipline of One-mind. Oneness empowers us; it affords impregnable knowledge. To cleave from it causes loss of cohesion in all undertakings; to lose it brings division in mind, and from there the loss of Tao. "Holding to the One" means overcoming the science of divisions.

Yet *Oneness* is only a word. It must be fully coordinated with truth, for they are reciprocal values and without each other are of only limited use. That is why we refer to the larger nature of meditative practice as "Observing Truth and Holding to the One." Holding to the One enables us to know truth, to direct our energy, to mindfully cultivate emptiness, and to guard our Self-nature and spirit. We must be continually mindful in our actions, for only by holding to the truth and to the great Oneness are the gates to the Way assured us.

> *Truth and Oneness are indivisible;*
> *Oneness cannot be cleaved from Truth.*
> *Truth and Unity—like trees and shade;*
> *Holding them firmly in mind*
> *With the Way as our guide*
> *We need seek no other path.*

CHAPTER SEVEN

Taoist Nature, Taoist Mind

Humanity's spiritual divisions, and they are many, concern themselves primarily with the concept of SelfRealization—Enlightenment—and how it is achieved. The intensity of our various divisions chiefly involves the degree of recognition and homage that individual traditions accord what to Taoists are known as the *Acquired* and *Intuitive* forms of knowledge used in leading the follower toward Self-Realization.

Heaven, the Pure Land, is impartial in its favors. How we attain its grace depends on our turn of mind and is not a matter for judgement. The way of heaven is deep and wide. Its truth is clear and just, and all things are cultivated and made manifest by its creativity. Yet beings are numberless, ideas are manifold, and we should not be surprised that the will of heaven is not clearly understood by everyone.

As human beings we long to reunite ourselves with the Supreme Way, the Way of Heaven. But heaven and earth are timeless; it is difficult to express the nature of our heart's deep yearning, and in our deliberations we are often obliged to use descriptive terms such as "the uncarved block," "the unborn state," or "intuitive knowledge." What do these terms really mean?

We are born possessing the primal energy of heaven and earth. To say that we are small worlds ourselves is not far from the truth. Yet our essence, energy, and spirit—the body's three precious elements—must be correctly coordinated in order to maintain its health and functions. All things under heaven—the seasons, the cycles of weather—also must change and readjust, for this is how heaven maintains its eternal face, and to follow the will of heaven we must take guidance from the Tao, the Way. The most appropriate method of doing so is to discard acquired preconceptions of the divine in favor of the intuitive mystery—"the unborn state" of *pre-reflective* consciousness. This is essential in the meditative linking of heaven and heart.

The loftiest of all Taoist ideals, "the unborn state" is a purely intuitive, pre-reflective awareness ordinarily conceived of as being a state of "no-mind," of silent, meditative attunement to the One-ment that is Tao—the great stillness at the core of both the inner and outer worlds. Taoists identify this "unthinking" state with the womb-like existence of an embryo: conscious, breathing, alive, but without thought or reflection. This primal condition of the unborn state, and other terms such as "the uncarved block," are emblematic of the essential Taoist concept of the great Void, which in Indic, Taoist, and Buddhist terms represents that from which all things are derived. So, in practice, following the way of heaven requires living with the fuller harmony of the Tao within our lives; with a spirit of fullness or completeness that is at once empty or devoid of "wanting-mind." This is intuitive knowledge.

"Acquired" knowledge by contrast is largely cognitive in nature and gained through adherence to doctrine, scripture, and ritual. Among Taoists it focuses on training the body's three precious elements through techniques that emphasize retaining body essences with the aim of condensing and distilling them for the purposes of health and longevity. These practices may lead to health but not necessarily toward purification and rectification of our heart, nor is real Taoist nature-wisdom realized in this fashion. So the desired "linking up of heaven and heart" can be made more difficult.

Taoists teach that the linking up of heaven and heart—of Tao-nature and Tao-mind (Buddha-mind)—is an arduous, lengthy road not suitable for everyone. Followers must be firm in commitment and resolve; they must study and practice at their discipline patiently and without sloth. Then, gradually, over a long time period, understanding comes that the higher realms of self-realization are not achieved without dedicated effort.

The first step in linking up self-nature with true Tao nature is purifying the heart until no trace of desire remains. If we are in sitting meditation we must detach ourselves from the external world, remaining lively, natural, and comfortable within. We can then guide our inner energy smoothly throughout the entire body, allowing it to circulate naturally, unceasingly, as freely as a flowing stream. No conscious thought is required. It is in the pulse and lightness of this moment we are able to realize the interbeing of our body, self-nature, and the universe as One.

Linking heaven and heart mirrors the tranquil brightness of water in heart and mind, as though our spirit were a sparkling crystal free of dust. At this level we begin experiencing other consciousness within our body, an awareness that dawns as effortlessly as the appearance of the morning star and which gathers in magnitude like a swarm of fireflies. This brightness cleanses both body and heart, replenishing our mind and spirit. It enjoins the dualities of our self-nature, a deeply profound achievement, and is a process that we can guide and utilize within our daily life, reaffirming continually our kinship with all of creation.

This communication with heaven, with Tao-nature, is arrived at naturally without strain or conscious effort. The Sages teach that this is the highest level to which we are able to apply ourselves, and though the results are mysterious, it is a process that can be properly analyzed. It is known for certain that calmness brings wisdom, and that wisdom in turn leads us toward the ineffable. Mindful of this, we must apply ourselves whole-heartedly to our meditation, whatever our individual path of practice.

Linking heaven and heart teaches a great deal: we come to know the smallness of our own place in Nature. We discover that practice is a personal undertaking, that there is no set path to follow. True self-realization is dependent purely on mindfulness in our ongoing daily activities and in our meditation, whether it be passive or dynamic. The means by which we express the will of heaven is ours alone to embrace.

The Way itself has always existed within; there is no need to seek it outside ourselves. By cultivating mindfulness in our daily actions, we discover that heaven is not really far away—it is within the heart.

Tao is the Way of Heaven;
The Way of Heaven, Tao.
Linking heaven and earth with sincerity
of purpose,
With skills honed through practice,
We come to learn the meaning of eternity.

CHAPTER EIGHT

Toward a Fuller Vision

Self-realization extends to everyone; we are all equal under heaven and, ultimately, individual goodness or evil is immaterial. Whatever our final path of practice, its ultimate purpose should be to lead us toward a better world. In this, every true path toward self-realization shares a common purpose. Different paths and faiths may remain distinct in their beliefs and methods, however, and each is likely to share conviction in the correctness of its own vision.

Every faith has the responsibility of clarifying doubt within the minds of its followers, although no single faith in particular should seek to exert hegemony of its doctrines to the detriment of another. Nor should it seek special favor or widely proselytize abroad its individual characteristics.

Taoism, which was to develop more slowly than Confucianism or Buddhism, and to have fewer followers in consequence, was first explicated by masters who in teaching the profound mystery of the Supreme Way advocated that their students research other paths, forswearing them never to criticize such faiths. Originally, it mattered little to which path a follower devoted himself or herself, for Taoism was not devoted purely to the middle way. Taoist sages valued the utility of other points of view, regarding them as other manifestations of the will of heaven.

Similarly, if we wish to work for the benefit of the world we must conduct ourselves above suspicion. This is most effectively achieved by not grasping for supremacy above others. True Taoism takes Lao-tzu's calmness and principle of inaction as its example of a natural-ly enlightened attitude. In broader terms, to truly benefit the larger community, we should politely make available whatever knowledge we possess that may be of use. It should be offered without deceit or thought of personal loss and gain.

∞

If we examine Confucianism, we find that following the Tang and Sung Dynasties its original content began merging significantly with Buddhism. The result was a Confucianism no longer entirely of itself: what remained became stylized—an academic abstract lack-ing in original meaning. This hybridized metaphysical form was criticized as lacking righteousness, and in time came to be viewed, especially in the West, as a Chinese "religion" having little to be cherished. Many modern Chinese also find this hybrid form inju-rious to the nation. It now seems likely that formal Confucianism is truly dying, since contemporary masters have not arisen to inher-it and renew its precepts—a tragedy, since the Confucian path has been so closely related to China's history for thousands of years.

A study of Confucianism and Taoism clearly establishes that the two have influenced each other considerably in many areas. Similarly, Buddhism and Taoism share a lengthy history of cross-fertilization of ideas, and this special relationship should be main-tained and fostered. Divisions do remain among existing schools—some stressing meditation and formal precepts, others focusing on commentary and theory—and this has led to different approaches, but further understanding and clarification of each school's fundamental truths should be encouraged.

We must remember that both positive and negative spiritual inte-grations are possible, too. Negative integrations star the paths of superstition or charismatic attraction and should be regarded with caution. But as profound changes in the world occur, as truth con-tinues to be refined—or if heaven presents us with new ideas—we are obliged to acknowledge them accordingly. Our human task is to seek truth, allowing for flexibility and understanding to refine and shape new situations as they arise. If wise new ideas may help us realize the will of heaven, naturally we should embrace them in improving ourselves as changes and circumstance oblige.

> *The Supreme Way is like the sea;*
> *It embraces every stream.*
> *Practice Oneness;*
> *Truth comes naturally:*
> *No competition, no trumpetry,*
> *Only the fusing of right ideas,*
> *Equally, harmoniously*
> *Rectifying the world.*

CHAPTER NINE

The Way of Compassion

One essential aspect of the Buddha dharma teaches us that all sentient beings exist within the world of illusion and delusion—*samsara*. The *samsara* of the present, though, is influenced by *karma*, the consequences of our past and present deeds. *Karma* is a principal factor in shaping the destiny of our present and future lives, and its influence upon the Great Wheel of death and rebirth should renew emphasis on the critical need for self-realization in our lives.

Buddhism recognizes the human condition is emblematic of all sentient beings; they are one and the same. If we are to attain peace with the world, we must also arrive at peace with all earthly elements. This quintessential Buddhist point of view finds correspondence in the Confucian notion that correction of the world's ills begins with the correction of human behavior. Confucianism asserts that whatever demons exist in the world do so as a consequence of our own rude and violent behavior. It is believed that if humanity's darker nature can be controlled through self-discipline and education, then evil has no place to root. This begs the question, however, of what to do with individuals of a fundamentally bad nature, and this critical problem of extending mercy to evil-minded persons is one that sages from the time of Yao and Xun* have found difficulty in resolving.

---

* The first recorded sage-kings in Chinese history, approx. 2255 B.C.

Buddhism addresses this difficulty through the ideas of karma and reincarnation. The value of these theories in discouraging harmful acts is generally useful, but in reality their influence has been weak upon those of evil-minded nature.

Taoism differs from both Confucianism and Buddhism on this matter. Like Confucians, Taoists begin with morality, seeking neither to draw attention to themselves nor to pursue actions out of the ordinary. While they wish to save humanity from human folly, as the wise fables note, "*Only the Old Fool Moves the Mountain*," and "*Only the Jingwei Bird Fills the Sea with Pebbles.*" Taoists are not conditioned to seek swift achievements; they work patiently, step by step, to reach their goal.

Taoism has its own way and order, preferring to cultivate small numbers who then educate others in their turn. In this way, the needs of the majority of the people are eventually served. Taoism temporarily sets aside the majority for the benefit of the truly committed, upon whom it concentrates all its educational energy.

True followers of Tao do so without ambition. Although some who thirst for recognition may progress sufficiently to become true Taoists, they are few. It is better that those with the potential for acquiring deeper wisdom be first encouraged. Again, while this method does not illumine large numbers quickly, the education of others must be effected realistically.

Taoism offers the contentment of moderation and the pleasures of privacy. Its sense of limitations suggests directions to us that are most likely to be free of danger or encumbrance. When decay and despair are abroad in the land, and humanity's search for answers and truth grows more ardent, such virtues come to seem like blessings. To those yearning for wealth, Taoism, like Buddhism, offers the teaching of mindful labor, and of possession without undue or aggressive attachment. To those yearning longevity it offers *Wu-wei,*

---

* These fables tell of a determined old man who moves a mountain blocking the path to his house; and of a King who in revenge for his son's drowning transforms himself into a bird and endlessly carries pebbles trying to fill up the sea.

teaching that only by not striving for such things can they actually be achieved. It returns us to nature, to simplicity and the middle way—Taoism's most profound and healing medicine.

Taoism's ultimate aim is attainment of the celestial realm—the holy land—in both its heavenly and human dimensions. This cannot be achieved through pure meditative practice alone; it is a matter of cumulative merit, and the means by which we come by this merit is also the means by which we may contribute meaningfully to the world.

> *This mortal world is vast;*
> *Lives transpire in adversity*
> *Longing to be saved,*
> *And there is a way.*
> *Without haste, without markings,*
> *In staying true to the wisdom of nature,*
> *We attain endless grace.*

CHAPTER TEN

Perfecting the Wisdom of the Heart

We are placed in Nature by Creation, and as such cannot be separated from it. The bonds are inextricable. Yet we continue to despoil the natural world—this essential component of our own vital being—by confusing it with our own personal ideas of what "nature" ought to be. Can this lead to anything but folly?

Knowing nature is knowing the great Way, the holy Tao. Maintaining harmony with nature increases both our wisdom and our ability to unite with and embrace nature in our daily lives.

Developing our relationship with nature, we cultivate noticeably greater skills in tracing the subtle meteorological influences of heaven and earth in our daily affairs. We may find our ability to deal with the broader matters of human nature in a just way is also improved. Often, we may sense our inner spirit seemingly uniting us with Oneness greater than ourselves.

∞

Knowledge is given us to use for our personal benefit and for that of the larger community, but it is seldom exercised fully by everyone. The truly wise are few; hence wisdom has come to be highly valued by every society. Wisdom, though, is something that can be both acquired and lost, and there is no lack of examples of the latter instance in the human tapestry.

Wisdom is something acquired gradually through observation of the infinitely rich patterns of the Earth. For this reason, such knowledge has come to be known as nature-wisdom, or the Wisdom of the Heart.

Those who treasure this knowledge find it evolves further when cultivated through a meditative practice. There are many such practices from which one can choose. "Meditative practice" by its very nature suggests a path which cultivates mindfulness or attentiveness as an essential part of its expression.

The longer we cultivate the wisdom of the heart within ourselves, the deeper we find its richness and the effectiveness of its application. Its spiritual power nurtures our entire physical body and maintains the balance of our vital essences, energy, and spirit. It exerts significant power upon both mind and body. This is an internal development and a matter for reflection; however, we must remember that in correctly attuning our own Self-nature we must first embrace the emptiness of the unborn state.

∞

Among Taoists, self-realization gained by study of the Supreme Way is called wisdom. The more firmly we apply ourselves to our meditative practice, the more our "wisdom root" grows—the more fully is self-realization experienced. Experiencing Tao-mind affords us an unaffected pleasure that may help balance the disaffections brought about through material desire. Tao-mind or Buddha-mind is a condition of awareness described by the Buddha as being "free of form," or a state of emptiness beyond the everydayness of this dusty world.

This experience of self-realization cleanses and renews the body through the regenerative healing power of our own inner spring. Our physical being becomes infused with the three precious elements of truth, spirit, and emptiness, and our internal energy resonates as clear as crystal, as bright as diamond. This *prajna*-energy is the union of self-nature with primal Tao, or pure Buddha-nature. Achieving this level of self-awareness is the very hearthstone of

Taoism and is as fundamental as breath to all Taoist arts including *Tai Chi*, calligraphy, and the healing and mantic arts.

Realizing Tao-nature within our own self-nature enriches our body and spirit alike. Within them are joined all truths without contradiction, for when heaven and our human heart are truly linked, both the will of heaven and the great Way of nature—the Supreme Way—may be freely observed without distraction. Our spirit is capable of travelling a thousand miles with the ease of light entering a room.

Attaining and perfecting Tao-nature frees us from the confinements of body and mind. Our actions and emotions pour forth freely, naturally, and without force. Those who cherish this state of awareness cling to neither Yes nor No in their livelihood, attire, or nourishment. They wear what clothing suits their disposition no matter the season or occasion; they may eat and drink many times during the course of a day, or nothing at all for days on end. They may sleep for days or not at all for many nights. They may walk a hundred miles in a day or sit still for days, months, or years. Their manner may be serious or carefree, silent or jocular. No conscious behavior governs their conduct; they behave, in short, in a completely natural way, beyond convention. We may say that, spiritually, these people are in an active state of *Wu-wei*.

Once the higher heights of Taoist wisdom have become familiar to us, certain physical detachments of soul, spirit, or body become possible in an entirely natural way. Through meditative control, our soul may detach from our body to travel widely. This natural occurrence is sometimes wrongly referred to as a separation of mind and body. What in fact transpires is that the soul may manifest itself directly to our sensory rather than customary intuitive perception— a phenomenon caused by the natural but intensified circulation of our *chi*, or life energy.

Once our soul is no longer compelled to stay in the material world, even in an enlightened body, it may discard the physical shell and reside alone. At this stage, our soul can live without corporeal form. It may also return to the mortal world within another physical body in need of certain spiritual fulfillment. Dependent on its condition and predisposition, our soul may be reborn in this fashion. It is a completely natural phenomenon.

The great Way is boundless and we are obliged to practice unceasingly with resolve and commitment. Regardless of our religious inclination, the final goal is the same: the Confucian strives to enter the Hall of the Sages; Buddhists work to reach *Sukhavati*, the Pure Land; and Taoists work toward the Celestial Realm. Yet we must remember that while we may achieve higher levels of self-awareness, this is not a guarantee that we ourselves are to become celestial. Once attuned to Tao-nature, we must practice ever more diligently and faithfully than before. The records of previous celestials prove that hardship remains even after achieving deep insight into the wisdom of Tao-nature. The measure of our practice at this stage must become the perfection of the unborn, uncarved, ideal state of existence, and we must be guided by this in both our meditation and our practice.

Although the physical body may suffer from the hardships of spiritual training, our soul grows and heals ever more steadily and harmoniously for such discipline. This is knowledge only fully understood and appreciated by those who are engaged in mindful study and practice of a spiritual path such as cultivation of the Supreme Way. It is indeed a great learning for the true path never ends.

> *Wisdom and Tao-nature:*
> *Their unity brings Inspiration.*
> *From mindful practice comes Self-realization.*
> *The Supreme Way, the unborn state,*
> *Is not far from hand.*

Rounded dates are approximate.

B.C.

2852   Fu Hsi originates trigrams and hexagrams which form basis of *I Ching*.

Approximate period of Yellow Emperor

2357   King Yao

2255   King Xun

c. 1700   *I Ching* use recorded on bamboo strips; origins of Chinese writing

1132–31   While imprisoned, King Wen writes explanations to Judgements & Images of *I Ching*

1000   Beijing founded

640   First School of Laws, China

c. 570   Lao-tzu born

551   Confucius born

501   According to Taoist legend, Lao-tzu and Confucius meet

c. 490   Lao-tzu dies

479   Confucius dies

c. 440   Mo-tzu introduces idea of utopian, communal state

c. 400   Concept of zero used in Chinese mathematics

398   Lieh-tzu first recorded living at Cheng

c. 390   Chuang-tzu born

358   Lieh-tzu dies

c. 320   Chuang-tzu dies

221   Emperor Huang-ti completes building of Great Wall

213   Great burning of books—especially those of Confucius and followers—under Huang-ti

202 Beginning of illustrious Han Dynasty under Liu Pang

150 Confucianism mandatory for Civil Servants

122 *Huainanzi* composed by scholars under King Liu An, synthesizing the Taoist traditions of both Lao-tzu and Chuang-tzu

100 Ssu-ma Chi'ien writes history of Chinese culture

A.D.

65 During reign of Ming-ti, a deputation is sent to India, who on their return establish Buddhist doctrine in China

79 *Discourses of Confucius* fixed in standardized form by Imperial decree

165 Emperor Huan makes historic official offering to Lao-tzu

166 Roman contact with China through silk trade

230 Tea introduced in China

284 Second Roman embassy to China

590 Wood-block printing introduced, China

c. 600 "Six Confucian Classics" become basis of Chinese Civil Service examinations

620 Tang Dynasty (620–906) fosters great poetic revival; Chinese sovereignty over more than eighty Asiatic peoples

c. 750 First daily newspaper, China

c. 850 Buddhism flourishes after Huang Tsang's journeyto India, but is later suppressed as a threat to Confucianism

c. 1100 Height of Southern Sung Dynasty (A.D. 960–1279); pleasure-seeking society evolves; flowering of arts and

Badiner, Allan Hunt, ed. *Dharma Gaia: A Harvest of Essays in Buddhism and Ecology.* Berkeley: Parallax Press, 1990. A landmark collection including work by Thich Nhat Hanh, Gary Snyder, Joanna Macy, Robert Aitken, and others, with a foreword by H.H. the Dalai Lama.

Burtt, E.A., ed. *The Teachings of the Compassionate Buddha.* New York: New American Library, 1955. Early discourses on the Dhammapada and later basic writings.

Carolan, Trevor, & Chen, Bella, trans. *The Book of the Heart* by Loy Ching-Yuen. Boston: Shambhala, 1990. Poetic transliterations of Master Loy's meditations on rectifying the heart.

Chang, Chung-yuan. *Creativity and Taoism: A Study of Chinese Philosophy, Art, and Poetry.* New York: Harper & Row, 1970. Excellent.

Conze, Edward, trans. *Buddhist Wisdom Books.* London: Unwin, 1988. Contains translations of the Diamond Sutra and the Heart Sutra. Authoritative.

Dalai Lama of Tibet. *Ocean of Wisdom.* Toronto: McClelland & Stewart, 1989. A heartwarming compendium of guidelines for living.

Dhammapada. The Cunningham Press edition: Alhambra, California, 1955. This is a lovely volume of the Buddha's fundamental teachings.

Dasho Nakchung. *Importance of Retribution in Human Life According to Buddhist Philosophy.* Thimphu, Bhutan: Royal Government of Bhutan Press, 1972. Charming and enlightening discourses in the Tibetan tradition.

Eido, Shimano Roshi, ed. *Like a Dream, Like a Fantasy: Zen Writings and Translations of Nyogen Senzaki..* Tokyo: Japan

Publications, Inc., 1978. Delightful teishos, notes, and ephemera from this seminal West Coast Zen sage.

Gia-Fu Feng and Jane English, trans. *Tao Te Ching of Lao Tsu.* New York: Vintage Books, 1972. A wonderful edition.

Govinda, Anagarika Lama. *Creative Meditation and Multi-Dimensional Consciousness.* Wheaton, Illinois: Quest Books, 1976. An exhaustive documentation of meditative phenomena. Quite breath-taking in scope.

Govinda, Anagarika Lama. *The Way of the White Clouds: A Buddhist Pilgrim in Tibet.* Berkeley: Shambhala, 1970. Brilliant scholarship on the Vajrayana tradition by a heartwarming teacher.

Guiness, Os. *The East, No Exit.* Downers Grove, Illinois: InterVarsity Press, 1974. A sharp Christian critique of expanding Western interest in Eastern mystic traditions, ironically offering considerable insight into them.

Hamill, Sam, trans. *Night Traveling: Poems from the Chinese.* Turkey Press, 1985. Fine translations of Li Po, Tu Fu, Wang Wei, and others. An elegant edition.

Hamill, Sam, trans. *Wen Fu: The Art of Writing by Lu Chi.* Portland: Breitenbush Books, 1987. A definitive edition.

Harris, Victor, trans. *A Book Of Five Rings by Miyamoto Musashi.* Woodstock, New York: Overlook Press, 1974. Essential.

Merton, Thomas. *The Way of Chuang Tzu.* New York: New Directions Books, 1965. An eclectic, engaging compendium.

Parrinder, Geoffrey, ed. *The Wisdom of the Early Buddhists.* New York: New Directions, 1977. Contains useful stories of the Buddha's life.

Payne, David. *Confessions of a Taoist on Wall Street.* New York: Ballantine, 1984. An astounding popular novel tapping the heart of Taoist practice in its exploration of "the Tao within the Dow-Jones." Excellent.

Reps, Paul, *Square Sun, Square Moon*. Rutland, Vermont, and Tokyo: Tuttle Books, 1974. Off-center vignettes. Useful.

Reps, Paul, ed. *Zen Flesh, Zen Bones*. New York: Anchor Books; Charles Tuttle edition, 1974. Irreplaceable gathering of Zen parables. Compiled with Nyogen Senzaki.

Rexroth, Kenneth, trans. *One Hundred Poems from the Chinese*. New York: New Directions, 1971. Roots collection by the elder of the West Coast's East/West literary tradition.

Rowland, Benjamin, Jr. *Art in East and West*. Boston: Beacon Press, 1964. Insightful discussion of aesthetics East and West. Very good.

Sakaki, Nanao. *Break the Mirror*. San Francisco: North Point Press, 1987. Quintessential Zen poems from Japan's memorable dharma-hobo, with a foreword by Gary Snyder.

Snyder, Gary, trans. *The Cold Mountain Poems of Han-shan*, from *Riprap and Cold Mountain Poems*, Farrar, Straus Giroux, 1990. The definitive translation.

Snyder, Gary. *The Practice of the Wild*. San Francisco: North Point Press, 1990. A magnificent collection of essays embracing traditional nature-wisdom within the context of contemporary environmental thought.

Stevens, John, trans. *One Robe, One Bowu: The Zen Poetry of Ryokan*. New York and Tokyo: Weatherhill, 1977. An excellent, definitive edition.

Sun Tzu. *The Art of War*. An indispensible Taoist masterwork. The Thomas Cleary translation is superb (Boston: Shambhala Dragon edition, 1988). James Clavell's 1983 Delacorte edition is a useful, interesting abridgement also.

Suzuki, D.T. *The Zen Monk's Life*. New York: The Olympia Press, 1972. An essential guide.

Suzuki, Shunryu. *Zen Mind, Beginner's Mind*. New York and Tokyo: Weatherhill, 1970. An essential introduction to Zen.

Van de wetering, Janwillem. *The Empty Mirror*. New York: Pocket Books, Simon & Schuster, 1973. An account of the author's experiences in a Kyoto Zen monastery. Useful.

Van de wetering, Janwillem. *A Glimpse of Nothingness*. New York: Washington Square Press, 1974. The author's further adventures in an American Zen community.

Waley, Arthur. *The Analects of Confucius*. New York: Vintage Books; original Unwin edition, 1938. Essential.

Watson, Burton, trans. *The Complete Works of Chuang Tzu* New York: Columbia University Press, 1968. Definitive.

Watson, Burton. *Hsun Tzu: Basic Writings*. New York: Columbia University Press, 1963.

Watts, Alan. *The Way of Zen*. New York: Vintage Books, 1957.

Watts, Alan. *The Spirit of Zen*. New York: Grove Press, 1958. Both of Watts' introductions to Zen are excellent.

Wilhelm, Richard, trans. *I Ching*, or *Book of Changes*. London: Routledge and Kegan Paul, 1951. Of the many available editions, Wilhelm's establishes the standard by which all others are measured.